All Those Old Sayings

gabriella j. labelle

ISBN: 979-8-9902370-2-5

All Those Old Sayings

gabriella j. labelle

Table of Contents

Tears Of Joy

Fake laugh, Weird laugh, Quick laugh, Cheap
More laughs, Less laughs, Real laugh, Deep

He probably can't tell that was a fake laugh because
he genuinely thinks he's that funny.
Sex is like laughter. How long do I have to fake
laugh for this interaction to be over? My cheeks are
hurting from holding this position, and I'd rather be
anywhere away from this pretending.

But it would be more uncomfortable to be still and
or sitting, I mean silent. So I guess we'll both just
continue to make more awkward noises, awkward
conversation until this whole ordeal is over with.

I'm too far in, I laughed when it didn't feel good, I
mean when it wasn't funny. But more uncomfortable
would be the truth. So even though those were some
of the driest jokes I've ever heard, one of us will lie
at the end and say, "we have to do this again." Sex is
like laughter. Funny.

One of the best laughs I've ever had was with a
coworker. A coworker who I shared an inside joke
with. Everyone could see the fun but nobody knew
the punchline but us. A coworker who I now can't
look at during the meetings cause I'll see things other
than their powerpoint presentation. Other than the
improvements we need to make before our summer

vacation. Other than the goals for the next year. I'm sorry could you repeat that, I didn't hear, over that joke you told last night, I was too busy replaying it in my mind. Sex is like laughter.

And all you'll hear are the snorts and cackles of two coworkers that laughed a little too hard, that laughed a little too long, and that probably shouldn't laugh again lest one party starts to take the joke too seriously while the other continues to think of the joke as just friends, I mean just funny. Sex is like laughter.

Sometimes, you find yourself laughing alone. Sometimes you are your safest human, I mean safest humor. Because sometimes no one understands your jokes. Sometimes you need a quick laugh just to counter the stress in your day. So you browse the interwebs for something funny but that leaves you feeling hollow because no laugh can compare to one that is shared with another human. That soul communion will always be better than your favorite online porn, I mean online pun. Laughter should be with someone.

Because sex is like laughter but intimacy is like joy. Closeness. Nearness. Safety. Physicality is not necessary to enjoy the presence of another. The connection that you created wasn't based on your diaphragm raising, wasn't based on your abdomen shaking, wasn't based on any noise escaping your bodies. In fact your bodies had no contribution, decided to put the jokes aside until you all signed the constitution of every other emotion that comes with a meaningful union.

But better to be alone than with someone who tries to make you laugh when you don't find anything amusing. You don't find them funny and yet they're using your clear disinterest to try harder, going farther than your permission, taking your silence as invitation to tickle you, to continue their harassment.

"Ah come on, you know that's hilarious." If it was, I'd be cackling not disgusted with your hands happening down my lower back. I would invite the hilarity if it was anywhere to be found, cause at this point a bad joke would be better than you trying to unzip my gown.

"You don't know what humor is anyway, bitch." Now I am being berated because your comedy comes from cruelty and your twisted humor is birthed from hatred and your lack of empathy showcases your selfish state of mind.

Touching without consent, did you mean tickling, no touching without consent. Causing you hysteria and mania, distorted conversation and dissociation. And now you no longer laugh because you think things are funny, you laugh because you are scared to do anything else. Afraid that they'll see your disdain behind that smile. You laugh because the last time you didn't, you were made to against your will.

Sex is like sex. Laughter is like laughter. Laughter is like sex. And sex is like laughter. But just remember that sometimes sex is no laughing matter.

Make no mistake, when it comes time to perform, he needs to be better than the best comedian.
But he will not be him who mistook your body for a plaything, a gag. He will be a man. He will be better than that boy, and you will not look forward to laughing, you will look forward to crying tears of joy.

When Life Gives You Lemons

When Life gives you lemons, leave them as such,
whoever suggested mutilating a
perfectly good piece of fruit
had not learned to appreciate what's in their cup

When Life gives you lemons,
leave them as such
life didn't give you lemons
for them to be cut up

When Life gives you lemons,
appreciate their beauty,
appreciate their peel
sniff their sweetly sour scent

but when the times up
thank them for theirs
and return them to Life untouched

When Life gives you lemons, leave them as such,
whoever suggested mutilating a
perfectly good piece of fruit
had not learned to appreciate what's in their cup

Slow Burn

Maybe I am the slow burn.
Maybe I am the one my heart longs for.

That sitting, waiting patiently in the corner,
afraid to approach me, and mesmerized by my every
movement, and intoxicated by the sound of my
voice, and distracted by my gaze, and hoping to hold
my hand, and missing the smell of my shirt,
and writing me poetry about our imagined love story
is . . . me.

Maybe I am the slow burn.
Maybe I am the greatest love story that I am praying
will happen.

What if I'm, with every waking minute and every
working muscle, and every gifted breath,
I am dying for a second of my time. To be around
me for just a minute more, to be able to enjoy my
smile, even from afar.

What if I am hoping I notice me,
hoping I realize that I will die without my love, that
even an ounce would give me reason to live.

That to live without my love is not a life worth living,
that I would do anything. I would do anything. I will
give anything. Will become anything. Do anything.
Say anything. Say anything for me to choose me.

What do I have to do for me to choose me?
I would choose me. Anyone would be lucky to have
me.

Why am I not enough? As me, I feel I am not
enough.

Maybe I am the slow burn. Now, standing, once
patient in the corner, next to me, anticipatory,
mesmerized by my mind, and intoxicated by my
endless desire to create, holding my gaze, unable to
look away, reaching out to hold my hand, breathing
in the smell of my vanilla perfume and reciting me
poetry about our breathtaking love story is . . . me.

Love is a Roller Coaster Ride

Love has been a roller coaster I'm not tall enough to ride.

It started in high school. My height was an attraction. I gave off all the wrong signs, apparently perceived as a tree and labeled as "too tall to ride."

I know what you're thinking--how tall am I?
I'm 5'8" and three quarters of a dollar sign, fine.
With legs that extend, as you can clearly see, to no end.

I lied. I'm 5'9"
But 5'9" of the best bottle of mulled wine with cinnamon and tangerines inside. That's a drink they make in England during winter nights

I lived in London for 3 months and never once rode the Eye--that's reasonable, but I've lived in me for 25 years and still feel too short to try because

Love is a roller coaster I'm not tall enough to ride.
My hands, shaky at the thought, get sweaty by my side
            And my stomach, fluttering, decides
            We're going to stay down here
            On the ground
            Where we're alive.
            I'm scared.

What if he loves me and . . . I don't love me.
What if I never see myself as worthy?
What if we talk until twilight becomes sunshine?
What if we walk through our childhood trauma and
Unconventional family drama long past my 11
o'clock bedtime?
What if the roller coaster breaks at the top
and we're stuck?

What if, worst of all, we fall
Like actually fall, not in love, but from the height of
what we once thought love was.

What if we fall and when he calls I pretend I'm at
the mall buying a basketball 'cause I'm tall and how
long can I stall using words that rhyme with all so
that I don't have to admit that this love is in past
tense.

That I was already locked in,
that the roller coaster bar came across my lap, and
I knew there was no turning back when I heard the
first click of this contraption, emphasis on the trap.

Shunned by my family and friends for getting stuck
on a attraction that was based on an attraction.

What do you call a ride that has no traction, We call
that a slip and slide which is highly representative
of this relationship but the only waterpark that we
visited was the one created by my eyes.

No traction unless you're talking about the one that
follows sub . . .

In addition, how long can I stall using words that
rhyme with all so that I don't have to mention that
I'm really . . . 5'10."

Yes, indeed, I lied again because the seams have
pulled from my roller coaster dreams and lovesick
has already happened to me for a man that was . . .
5'3."

5'3" in character. 6 '4" in body.
5 '3" in morals. 6 '4" in wingspan.
5 '3" in meeting my parents.
6'4" in . . . all the other ways a 6'4" man can be.

Lengthy were the conversations that we had
regarding the fact that I didn't feel seen.
Wide were the wounds he had not yet healed from.
Wet was my face with tears after screaming as loud
as my lungs would allow.

Screaming as loud as my lungs would allow.
Loop-di-loop, round-and-round, upside down,
inside out. As loud as my lungs would allow, I
screamed.

I lost my voice by the end. Never again.

So instead of Love, I went a different direction.

Still trying to find excitement.
Still trying to find adventure.
Still trying to find a rush.

I walked a few paces to the kiddie ride that read,
"Crush."

On a good day I'm 5'11."
Either way, Love has been a roller coaster that
knocked me down a few inches and said, "I'm sorry,
hon, you're not tall enough to ride."

Hell-bent

But do you know what's crazier than death? I don't know because I haven't died. And you don't know because you are reading this poem. I don't mean this to sound like you should test the waters, or rather test the ground, but it does mean that I've never known if life is the better option.

This place is like a bag of socks, you never know which one you're gonna get. One day could be like a match made in heaven, the next could be a day full of holy craps.

This place is like drying your clothes. Sometimes they're wet.

This place is like the relationship I have with my mother--cold.

This place is like letting the love of your life get away--unaffordable.

This place is like the average of two people that hate each other--mean.

This place is like a card game--"They declare war."

This place is like being born--inevitable.

I am, you are, we are inevitable. And then told to be

grateful.

I didn't ask to be here.
But do you know why I stay? Because my niece
looked at me, and I smiled. She had just turned one.
I smiled and she didn't smile back. And I loved her
anyway, if not more.

She almost rolled off the couch and I cared, and I
felt, and I was moved, and I was grounded, and I
was made human. And I don't understand why but I
was supposed to be there. I am supposed to be here.

And holding her hands makes this place, the only
place I've ever known, worth knowing.

And do you know what's crazier than death? I don't
know and you don't know because you're reading
this poem.

But if I had to guess what was crazier than death, I'd
say living.

Fashion Victim

I am not actually the one in charge of the emotions
of my mother. I am not actually the one who needs
to soothe the shame of my sister. I am not actually
responsible for holding happiness to present to my
niece when I see her.

And I have been fired from carrying the weight of
my family's expectations.

And so, in my newly found free time, I try on
different personas to see how they fit

Some were too loose around the waist and
Required a constant hand at my hip
Others too tight and left unfavorable prints

Still others fit my body and not my style
And others fit my style but were too great an expense

So here I am, in the role I've always been
Dressed head to toe in the emotions of my mother,
The shame of my sister and the happiness I've laid
away for my niece.

Wanting simply to undress to begin to know who I
am

Underneath.

Hand-me-down

I am my favorite thing to put on in the morning
I am my favorite thing to wear out

I am my most comfortable clothing when it's raining
and I curl up on the couch

I feel prettiest in me.

But sometimes in the middle of the day,
in the midst of a conversation,

I begin to wear you
And I don't recognize until I come home
and look in the mirror

And realize I've changed.

Hung Out to Dry

Grief is a towel that has soaked up water over a
lifetime

And is then wrung out in an instant
important and inconvenient and
demands to be done right at this moment

Strong hands grip towel and twist in opposite
directions
Strong hands strain
Strong hands release for a moment
Strong hands readjust to get better grip

Again with the wringing, and twisting
towel loses water

Until weep slows to pour and pour to cry
Until water no longer makes heavy beating sound as
it beats the ground

Until all that falls are a few teardrops

Survivors Guilt

My sisters and I used to get ready together in the
bathroom

We hogged our corner of the mirror as best as we
could

Zipped and changed and traded our clothes
and passed the eye shadow back and forth
I didn't mean to leave them alone in the bathroom to
dress up

Except that dress up in this poem means lie.

The only reason I know they are still lying is because
I was also on the road to becoming a corpse bride

I say a corpse bride because another word for
chronic lying in order to protect yourself
is die.

I didn't mean to leave them alone in the bathroom to
dress up

Except that dress up in this poem means die.

Love-Hate Relationship

I love you
Here I love you means
Thank you for washing the dishes

I love you
Here, I love you means
You've been a good girl lately

I love you
Here, I love you means
You make me look good in front of
all the important people in my life
Of which, you are not one

I love you
Here, it means
You obey

I love you
You don't make mistakes

I love you
Your hair looks better when it's the way I like it

I love you
You are almost perfect

I love you
Just wait until your tummy is flat

I love you
Stop complaining

I love you

When my mother said she loved me,
she meant it.

We just didn't share the same definition.

And my father never meant anything he said.

So I love you was always conditional, or otherwise
just words we were taught to say after goodbye and
before bed.

Robbing the Cradle

The age at which I was allowed
to ask questions was cut short

Trauma will do that
Give you answers to all of life

Prematurely.

I wanted to be a cowgirl
then a spy
until I wanted to be a runaway
then safe

I grew up to be none of those
and I knew not to ask why

Trauma Bonded

Trauma bonded: intense feelings of connection
based on pain, abuse, and everything else that is not
love

Can you imagine?
Feeling so much energy in your body
that you mistake it for the good type of passion

Trauma bonded: a jester dressed up as love,
playing intimacy with a painted smiling face.
Playing family with hands covered in white gloves.
Faking safety while juggling knives that we pulled
outside of our backs and chests

Own Worst Enemy

Oh my gosh, she's so cool!

She is ice cold, keeping control, even when those
who know her, hold her at night. She is not alright
but doesn't weep, doesn't whimper, doesn't whine,
doesn't cry

Oh my gosh she's so strong!

She is in strongholds
chained to the shame of past woes.

She's so brave!

She is outraged, encaged, and swallowed whole by
her vices, sabotages any hopes of getting help
because in childhood she was left to her own devices.

She is so smart!

To project her heart, to be transparent, but not
vulnerable, to appear as open and connected is
honorable. but whats more twisted than lying about
your truth?

Oh my gosh, she's so pretty!

Believes herself to be pretty ugly.

Can't get enough compliments from dogs who wanna bone. Can't get enough friends to not feel alone.

She is lost in the world of lies she tells herself, while her body finds comfort in the sick habits of coping.

Call it sex, call it drugs, call it drink. Call it him, call it them, call it kinks. As long as its never called out, she is safe in the mess that she makes.

The decisions that take her down a path of self-destruction, and self doubt.

Oh my gosh she's so kind.

She is in binds, in battle against her mind. Oh my gosh she's so wise. She is dying inside.

Oh my gosh she's so me.
Oh my gosh she's so you too.

When are you going to realize cool, strong, brave, smart, pretty, kind, girl that being cool, strong, brave, smart, pretty, kind is not why those who love you, love you.

Those who love you, love you.

And that is the end of the statement because there is

no because.

There is no reason why they should consider
anything other than your existence as why.

When are you going to realize that you should love
you, and there is no because.

Curiosity Killed the Cat

Curiosity killed the cat
but having 9 lives, the cat bounced back.

Tried it again quite a few times
lost more lives
down to five.

Then learned from his mistakes
met curiosity face to face.

He said "everyone told me to fear my fate,
but I realized that conquering you would make me
great."

They'd have to rewrite that old saying
to something like

Curiosity killed the cat
but having 9 lives, the cat bounced back.

Class in Session

Life is like my third grade english teacher
It waits until I stop talking to give instructions

And I don't listen the first time
The second time I challenge its wisdom
The third time I whine that it's too hard

Life just waits until I stop talking
Then repeats the instructions

Death toll

I held the hand of my grandmother
when she passed away
and was scared at how much
of her was missing

I didn't know that the scariest part of death
was that they leave so much
of what should be them

Behind

Enough is Enough

When the eulogy was read, the tear wept,
and the body lowered into the ground,
they found a letter from the universe
that simply said, "enough."

For is there no greater definition for death?

And more tears flowed for them because
this enough was only granted for the one being
lowered.

And then another eulogy was read and another body
lowered.

And then another eulogy was read and another body
lowered.

Until another eulogy and another body.

And all the enoughs belonged to those lowered.

And none to those standing above them.

Simon Says

How are you not further into me
or I into you

When we've opened up all of ourselves to each other

Come closer
Simon says come closer

What is this thing called skin
this thing called body

That keeps our souls from touching

Touch me
Simon says touch me

Simon says

Dig your hands into my heart
And squeeze

While I wrap my arms around your safety
And hold on for dear life

Say it
Simon, say it

Love and War

There are wars in the world
And people dying
And all I want to do
Is write about love

But who says love is light
Who says the wars being fought
Are not over love

of power.
of money.
of people.

Sights and Smells

No one ever told me
it was important to
wash your sheets
after the person you love

Left them

So that their smell
didn't mix with your dreams
anymore

Maybe tomorrow
I'll wash your sweater

Leave Well Enough Alone

I love you too much to kiss you once
and not be able to kiss you for forever

So I will not kiss you once
to protect both our hearts

When we arrive at our inevitable departure

Nothing to Write Home About

I am not an anomaly
this didn't
this doesn't
this will not only happen to me

I am not an anomaly
as much as I want to be
for the attention, for the clout, for the individuality

I am not an anomaly

I am not the only one
more have come before
and more will come

This is something that

Has been done
 Has been done
  Has been done
   Has been done
    Has been done
     Has been done

Is happening

And will always be

This rubs me the wrong way, so I ask myself why I've

made my pain my identity

Out here crying and whimpering and praising my
pain, as if I'm an anomaly

For my pain can be found on every corner of the
globe

For I am not an anomaly

Distance Makes the Heart Grow Fonder

Distance makes the heart grow fonder
Distance makes the heart grow darker

Distance makes the heart grow in whatever direction
the heart was going before separation

I know you hate your father
Let's sit in that for a minute, it's easy to forget it
I'm going to repeat it
because sometimes I don't own it

Easier to lie and say love
But I know you hate your father
And you know you hate your father

Distance makes the heart grow fonder for
What you missed
What you wished
What you know doesn't and will never exist

Distance gives you space and time to heal
Helps you cook your meals

While you hope distance does its work to help your
father

Do what he said he would do
Do what he said he would do
"Do what you said you would do!"

But instead

Distance is your father

That sperm donor mocked me for having symptoms of bipolar

That he created

Distance makes the heart grow harder
Distance has made my heart grow darker

And mother? Where was she?
Mother "didn't know," "doesn't know,"
wasn't the best

Far from it, she claimed she was giving a hundred and ten percent

But how does that math work out when you have already emotionally left

Checked out as a result of unresolved traumas that you pass on to your daughters

Distance makes the heart grow farther
Blood is thicker than water

And where the blood flowed from your wounding words are scars that make maps to destinations that keep me protected from unkindred spirits

Blood brothers has a whole new meaning

Conversations with your siblings
to see how they're coping

With the reality that our parents' daily presence
didn't fix our emotional abandonment

If distance has made my heart grow fonder
it is for the safety that has been created by leaving

Distance has made my heart grow darker, colder
closed off to the possibility of returning

Distance has made my heart grow in the direction it
was already going before separation

Yearning, for the time when distance can retire
knowing that no amount of time, or space, or
distance will make my heart grow fonder

Home of the Brave

I don't want to be brave
Because brave has always meant alone
And I don't want to be alone
Because alone has meant unsafe

And I want to be safe
Because safe has meant peace
And I want peace
Because peace has meant no war

And I don't want war
Because war has meant

I must be brave

Flesh and Blood

My mother wears inflexibility
like a suit of armor.
She is an unchanging woman.
Proud of her coat of arms.

She is her mother's daughter.
Except unkind.

I had a conversation with
my father the other day.

I've had kinder conversations
with serpents. Better rapport with demons.
And more warmth from dead bodies.

He is no one's son.

I look like the mix of the two.

Fortunately, that is where the
resemblance stops.

Gut Feeling

Stop buying time
by asking God

As if his word will be final
when he has already
given you a body

That has screamed "stop!"
or has begged "go!"
and has reminded
over and over

You know
You know
You know

.

Different As Can Be

Why should green understand yellow
when yellow is yellow and green is not

Why should you understand me

When I am me
and you are green

You Live and You Learn

I hate giving advice
as if I've been here before
as if I've lived a life before

As if I've lived your life before

• *gabriella j. labelle* •

Essays

Rising from the Ashes

What happens to a butterfly when it first enters the cocoon? Why do we focus so much on the part of it coming out of its cocoon? Why do we not talk about how horrified a phoenix must be during the flames, we so quickly consider the moments after the flames.

How have we glamorized metamorphosis to the degree that we worship the miraculous deaths of these creatures. Holding onto the miraculous bit and completely ignoring the reality of death. Death. Death.

Death is the end of hope because hope suggests, nay requires, nay begs for life and so when death has come, we no longer hope for more, instead we grieve. We grieve because we have reached the end. So the butterfly emerges, the phoenix rises, not in beauty and power and strength.

They emerge and they rise in grief, confusion, fear, and trauma. They are worshiped and embraced but having a new form they do not recognize this embrace as love or acceptance. They interpret the embrace as more consuming flames or the suffocating shrinking of an already tight space.

They are not brave and fearless and respectable. They are confused, fearful, and traumatized.

To wish for metamorphosis is to first and chiefly wish for death. To wish for the end of hope. Only with the end of hope do we realize there's a greater power that sustains life after. What that power is, I cannot fully define.

But we know that the butterfly and the phoenix are not wishing for what they receive. But what they receive is greater than death and greater than hope, it is life anew.

In Sickness and in Health

Healing is not light. Healing is war. The way in which people discuss healing, it suggests that it is a process in which everyone is able to endure. That once engaged, the process will dictate its next steps and the only responsibility of the one who is to be healed is to hold on while the ride commences. No. That is not how Healing works. You must fight tooth and nail for Healing. It is not given, it is taken. Healing is fought for, fought over, stolen, lost.

Healing is one of the most precious commodities, standing next to time and love. And the reward for obtaining this precious commodity is seldom experienced when one first encounters it, when one first learns of it.

Healing, furthermore, is not knowing. Knowing, ofboth Healing and what one needs to heal from, can aid in understanding the necessary steps for Healing, but another common misconception is that awareness of the problem is the start of overcoming the problem.

Knowing is not healing. One can know the start line of a race and just as well not run. Healing is a seed. A seed that must be planted, that must be nurtured continuously. Healing has no plans of growing without the participation of the one who would most benefit. There's no shortcuts or naturally occurring processes that one can stumble upon. No. Healing is the most demanding exercise of the soul, of the body, of the mind, that produces the most rewarding gifts of life. Love, joy, peace. And just like all love, joy, and peace in this world, there is first war. How long? How much will need to be sacrificed? Will you survive? All of this is unknowable at the start, and remains unknowable through the journey. Which can simply be described as a most unfun voyage through uncertainty and near constant pain. A place in which no one in their right mind enters. An unnecessary expense save for those preparing to open the door to a physical death hoping for one final solution. No, Healing has never been light. Healing is war. But, if there ever was a war worth waging, it would be this one.

Reality Check

I didn't know that an answered prayer would come in the form of dissolution of my reality.

I'm not sure we plan for our worlds to fall apart in response to our desperation for revolution. And yet, there has been no other report of a better way of rebuilding than complete and under destruction of the original structure.

Why are we so flabbergasted when our lives are turned inside out and upside down right after declaring that we want our lives turned inside out and upside down. We are funny creatures. And are unaware of our requests until they are granted.

Knowing the path of destruction, would we still embark on the journey? If we had the capacity to fully comprehend what our requests asked of us, would we continue to ask for more? I'd hope we would. For there can only be one establishment at a time and without the relinquishing of the first, we obstruct the construction of the second.

How hypocritical of us to ask and then become angered by the reality that we must release in order to receive. How childish that we can't see full hands have little room to accept more, that full limbs have little space to embrace the next set of gifts.

We rather settle. Holding onto what we once held lightly now tighter. White knuckle grips wrapped around the very things we unknowingly asked to be removed.

I pray that our prayers remove that which we prayed for when it's time.

Reflection

_____

_____

_____

_____

_____

_____

_____

_____

_____

_____

_____

_____

_____

_____

_____

_____

_____

_____

_____

_____

_____

_____

_____

gabriella j. labelle

• all those old sayings •

BOOKS BY GABRIELLA J. LaBELLE

In No Particular Order
Quintessential Inquisitions

Excerpt from Gabriella J. LaBelle's Forthcoming Novel

". . . And the storm came! The people weren't ready for the revenge of Keturah. A wave with the ferociousness of the mighty gods themselves welled up on shore. The ancient Taigídan people said the wave shaped into a huge monster who used his giant fists to destroy everything in sight. Smash! Crash! Boom! Bang!"

Little voices, giggles and screams, carried into the hall as Makani Lumas dragged her travel bags and belongings into her room.

"Crash! Bang! Boom! He demolished home after home. As he walked, he left craters in the land. Each step causing earthquakes, flooding homes, and ripping trees right out of the ground!"

The comically deepened voice of her mother, even from a distance, felt more welcoming than the hug she received from her father. She couldn't see her yet, but she knew her mother was acting as the monstrous wave, tickling the littles while puffing up her cheeks with air and blowing out forcefully, mimicking the sounds of the winds and rains.

She missed this voice. This one that had lulled her to sleep with stories an incalculable amount of times. Makani had been away, had to be, to complete her

studies. But did she have to be away for the extra
two years? Could she not have visited more often,
not just during the festivals and special occasions?
"Makani, why are you reluctant to come home?
You are running from something, you are mi chan,
and I can feel you, even across oceans," this was the
recurring conversation.

"I'm not running from anything. If I want to be a
healer, I have to complete my studies," she assured
the voice and reassured herself in the process. She
was diligent each time the voice tried to convince
her to study closer to home or to take a longer break.
No, she would say, I have to stay focused, and I have
to stay away for my studies.

She walked across the hall and knocked quietly
before entering their room, she sat down at the end
of her younger brother's bed with her legs folding
underneath her. The room was as one would expect
for two eight year olds, loud with color and engaging,
each item begging for attention. Every article the
exact same but in a different hue.

Kai's towel, green, hung next to Kivi's purple towel,
on the back of the closet door. Kai's dresser, blue,
held a yellow lamp and Kivi's dresser, red, had an
orange lamp of the same shape. Because if one
gets a lamp, they both get a lamp, disregarding the
function and excess of light completely.

Their two beds were separated by a small wooden

table with yet a third lamp in between that shone
just enough to create big shadows on the wall behind
their mother as she transformed into the ancient
characters. When Makani settled, their mother, still
using an artificially deep voice, continued to oscillate
between standing at the end of the beds and sitting
at the foot of Kivi's bed, arms waving all the while as
she continued her destructive path.

"Keturah's plan to destroy the island had succeeded,
and all the people were wiped from the face of the
island," their mother got quiet and put on a face of
sadness momentarily.

"Except!" she suddenly shouted loudly and all three
of her children jumped, "except that Keturah was
wrong! She was not prepared for the amazing and
powerful Kaitan and Akiva."

She used a triumphant voice when announcing
their names, elongating syllables, and the twins cheer
at hearing their roles in this story as, per usual, the
heroes.

"They hid themselves during the worst of the storm.
Despite the monster sent by the goddess and despite
his destruction, all of the people were saved and
protected by the courageous Kivi and Kai, who
rescued every family and borrowed fire from Zuka to
fight the wind and the waves.

Day and night, wading through the waters that

drowned the island, Kai and Kivi," their mother always took care to switch the order in which she said their names to ensure one is not always mentioned first, "took the powerful fire and fought the floods until they receded. Alas, they defeated Keturah and her monster, letting all of the people return and rebuild their island." More cheering and triumphant laughter.

"That's what he gets!" Kivi swung her fist in the air. "We will defend the island forever!" Kai, standing on his bed, jumped up and landed on his back, earning a stern look from kan.

"And exhausted from the Water Wars," their mother continued, "they laid their heads down." At this part, she raised her eyebrows to suggest that they should now be listening very carefully and following the actions in the story. "They laid their heads down upon their pillows." Some pillows were swapped here and there, a blanket was pulled up only to be thrown off the body completely. She waited until they both got under the covers after a few futile protests.

"And closed their eyes." Again, she waited while Kai blinked numerous times, claiming that his eyes were technically closed because of how fast he's blinking. "And closed their eyes," she said more sternly this time. "Turned out their lights," she rose and circled through the room, turning out one, two, three lights. Stars cut on above when the light of the lamps retired, "got a kiss from their kan."

"And a hug from their han," Makani said as she laid on top of each of them in turn, tickling them until they screamed and complained about not being able to breathe. When they resettled, their mother finished saying, "and slept peacefully."

GABRIELLA J. LaBELLE is an avid storyteller, and a multidisciplinary writer and performer. Her work is rooted in soul-stirring stories and internal transformation.

At the heart of her artistic vision is a deep commitment to using language as a catalyst for introspection and connection.

Whether on the page or the stage, Gabriella's writing invites readers and listeners alike to pause, feel, and reflect.

She resides in Washington, DC.

All Those Old Sayings is her third publication and her second collection of poetry.

www.ingramcontent.com/pod-product-compliance
Lightning Source LLC
LaVergne TN
LVHW041232080426
835508LV00011B/1176